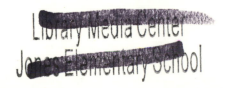

Revolutionary
Poet

Revolutionary Poet

A Story about Phillis Wheatley

by Maryann N. Weidt

illustrations by Mary O'Keefe Young

A Carolrhoda **Creative Minds** Biography

Carolrhoda Books, Inc./Minneapolis

To teachers and librarians. You make books come alive.

The author wishes to thank the staff of the Boston Public Library, the Boston Athenaeum, and the Massachusetts Historical Society. Special thanks to Mr. Peter Drummey.

This book is available in two editions:
Library binding by Carolrhoda Books, Inc.
Soft cover by First Avenue Editions
c/o The Lerner Publishing Group
241 First Avenue North
Minneapolis, Minnesota 55401 U.S.A.

Library of Congress Cataloging-in-Publication Data

Weidt, Maryann N.
    Revolutionary poet : a story about Phillis Wheatley / by Maryann
N. Weidt ; illustrations by Mary O'Keefe Young.
        p.   cm. — (Carolrhoda creative minds book)
    Includes bibliographical references and index.
    ISBN 1-57505-037-4 (lib. bdg.)
    ISBN 1-57505-059-5 (pbk.)
    1. Wheatley, Phillis, 1753–1784—Biography—Juvenile literature.
2. Afro-American women poets—18th century—Biography—Juvenile literature. 3. Women slaves—United States—Biography—Juvenile literature.
[1. Wheatley, Phillis, 1753–1784. 2. Poets, American.
3. Slaves. 4. Afro-Americans—Biography. 5. Women—Biography.]
I. Young, Mary O'Keefe. II. Title. III. Series.
PS866.W5Z93   1997
811'.12—dc21
[B]   97-1566

Manufactured in the United States of America
1 2 3 4 5 6 – MA – 02 01 00 99 98 97

Table of Contents

1

She Had No Name

Though the day was hot and humid, the dark-skinned child stood on the Boston dock and shivered. For clothing she wore a piece of dirty carpet. She spoke no English. She did not know where she was, but she knew she had traveled many days on a ship so crowded with people that many of them had died. Some had died of hunger, for on the ship there was only rice to eat and little water to drink. Some died of disease. Some, if they found the chance, threw themselves overboard and drowned.

The slave ship *Phillis* had arrived in Boston, Massachusetts, on July 11, 1761, with seventy to eighty young African women and children aboard. The girl was one of these.

From her size, and the fact that she had lost her two front teeth, the child appeared to be about seven years old. No one knew her age for sure. She had been snatched from her family in Africa and brought to America to be sold as a slave.

As she stood in the bright sunlight, she remembered her mother pouring water each morning to welcome the sun. This was a Muslim custom, practiced by the Fula people in West Africa. The written language of the Fula was Arabic. At home in Africa, the child had probably begun learning to write.

Slave trading was big business in Boston. A ship would leave the harbor packed with coffee, sugar, tobacco, guns, fish, or even horses. Sailing to the West Indies, the traders would exchange these goods for rum. Then, moving on to Africa, they would trade the rum for men, women, and children who would be taken back to New England and sold as slaves.

Nearly six hundred slaves lived in Boston in the mid-1700s. Most were house servants. In Massachusetts, slaves were called "servants for life." That meant that they were owned by a master just as horses and cattle were owned. In the northern colonies, slaves had a few rights—they could bring lawsuits and own some property.

Whenever a trader had slaves for sale, he advertised in the local newspaper. Such a notice appeared in the *Boston Gazette* of July 29, 1761. It read: "To Be Sold; A Parcel of likely Negroes, imported from Africa, cheap for cash, or short credit; Enquire of John Avery."

Like most well-to-do Bostonians, John and Susanna Wheatley owned a number of slaves. Susanna read the notice and thought about her own slaves. They were old and weak. Susanna, at the age of fifty-two, wanted a strong young girl to help with household chores. After all, the Wheatley home on King Street was large. Some called it a mansion.

John Wheatley made a good living as a tailor. He also owned a shop on King Street where he sold wine, tea, and candles. In addition to his home and store, John owned a two-hundred-ton, three-masted merchant schooner called the *London Packet.* He also had several warehouses, wharves, and other houses he rented out.

As Susanna stood on the dock fanning herself, she could see that the child standing before her was young but obviously not strong. Still, Susanna felt sorry for the child, and so she chose her. One of Susanna's relatives later wrote that Susanna was swayed by the "modest demeanor and the interesting features of the little stranger."

John Wheatley paid John Avery about ten pounds sterling—less than the price of a silver cream pitcher—for the sickly child. Avery was happy to be rid of her. He feared she might die before he sold her, so he gave Wheatley a very good bargain.

Leaving the dock with the girl in tow, Susanna noted the name of the slave ship: *Phillis*. She named her new servant Phillis, after the ship that brought her to the colonies. Like the family's other slaves, Phillis's last name would be Wheatley, the same as her owners.

John wrapped a blanket around Phillis's narrow shoulders and motioned for her to climb into the carriage. Phillis had never seen a horse or a carriage. She stepped gingerly around the strange-looking animal. When Prince, Mr. Wheatley's driver, saw that his master, his mistress, and the child were ready, he signaled the horse to proceed.

On the way to the Wheatley home, Phillis peeked out from under the blanket. She spied oxen pulling carts of lumber down the street, the drivers shooing chickens and hogs out of the way as they went. She heard strange-sounding words, as men and children, seeking work as chimney sweeps, sang: "Sweep 'em down, ladies; sweep 'em down to the ground."

She wrinkled her nose at the smell of imported British teas and coffees from shops along the way. From the taverns, the scent of West Indian rum and imported pipe tobacco wafted out. One odor, however, hung like a cloud over Boston. It was fish—mackerel, cod, lobster, and even shark. Boston was the center of the New England fishing industry.

King Street, where the Wheatleys lived, was the busiest street in Boston. It joined directly with Long Wharf, where ships bringing goods to the town docked. At one end was the Old Colony House, where much of Boston's business took place. One block north was Faneuil Hall, where town meetings often went on far into the night. Also located on and near King Street were eight booksellers, ten printers, and several newspaper publishers.

John and Susanna Wheatley were churchgoing Congregationalists. They attended the New South Church, where they had been married on Christmas Day, 1741. All five of their children were baptized there. Sadly, only two of the children had survived— twins named Nathaniel and Mary.

Eighteen-year-old Mary Wheatley was delighted to have Phillis in the house and treated her like a little sister. Mary wanted to be a teacher, so she set about teaching Phillis to read and write.

Phillis was an eager student. Within a few months, she learned to speak and read English. Susanna saw to it that she read the Bible, both the Old and New Testaments. Before long she was reading every book in the Wheatley home. She was lucky the Wheatleys owned plenty of books. When she finished those, she explored the libraries of wealthy Bostonians who were friends of the Wheatleys. She even borrowed books from Thomas Hutchinson, the governor of Massachusetts. At some point in all this reading, Phillis began wanting to write down her own words.

One day Phillis found a piece of charcoal and wrote on the brick wall of her room. She was so proud of what she had written—she couldn't wait to show Mary. Mary ran to tell her mother. Mrs. Wheatley was not angry. She, too, was proud of Phillis's gift for learning. But from then on, she made sure Phillis had plenty of writing paper and quill pens.

Mary taught Phillis to read ancient Greek and Latin, and she guided Phillis to ancient writers in those languages. Phillis discovered a Latin writer named Ovid. Within a few years, she was not only reading his stories but translating them into English as well. She also translated long story poems by the Greek writer Homer. Every day she studied geography, astronomy, and ancient history.

And she read poetry. Her favorite poet was the British writer Alexander Pope. He wrote long poems called elegies, which usually honored a person who had died. Phillis also loved Pope's translations of Homer's works. From reading Pope's work, she learned about the rhythm of poetry.

As the years went by, the young girl Susanna had bought as a servant spent more time reading and writing than dusting a table or toting a bucket. The Wheatleys were kind to all their slaves, but Susanna grew to love Phillis almost as her own child. She did not think of Phillis as an ordinary slave. When Phillis was sick—she often suffered from asthma—she was sent to the country for rest. This treatment of a slave was practically unheard-of.

Phillis came to occupy a special place in the Wheatley household. Unlike the other slaves, who lived in the carriage house, Phillis had her own attic room with heat and light. Next to her bed, Susanna provided a quill, ink, paper, and a lighted candle, so Phillis could write down her thoughts if she awoke during the night. Phillis's young mind was so busy that if she waited until morning to write down an idea, she might lose it.

Also unlike the other slaves, Phillis ate her meals with the family, except when they had company. Then she sat at a separate table. Phillis may have been special, but it was never completely forgotten that she was a slave.

Phillis often saw Susanna writing letters to her friends, so Phillis began to write letters, too. When she was eleven, she wrote her first letter. It was to

Susanna's friend the Reverend Samson Occom, who was lecturing in Britain. Reverend Occom was a traveling preacher. Susanna often sent him money to support his missionary work.

Phillis liked writing letters, but she wanted another way to express her feelings. When she was about twelve, she began to make up poetry. The first poem that Phillis remembered writing was "On the Death of the Rev. Dr. Sewell when Sick, 1765." Reverend Joseph Sewall (Phillis misspelled his name) was pastor of the Old South Church, which Phillis attended. Reverend Sewall was not dead when Phillis first wrote the poem. But he was sick—so sick that he had to be carried to the pulpit in a chair. He lived another four years, and Phillis rewrote the poem at least four more times. It was an elegy, the kind of poem she had read by Alexander Pope.

Phillis found ideas for poems in what she heard and saw around her. In the Wheatley home, religion was an important part of everyday life. Phillis wrote a great deal about religious ideas and feelings in both her letters and her poems. She also found inspiration on the streets of Boston. Although as a slave, Phillis could not be a citizen, she watched as citizens resisted British rule. The American colonists wanted to be free to rule themselves.

On August 14, 1765, as Phillis sat at her desk reading or writing, she heard a clamor of angry voices outside her window. Looking out, she recognized several King Street merchants—publishers, printers, and booksellers. They were shouting, "Liberty! Property, and no Stamps!" Phillis knew, as all of Boston knew, the cause of their anger—the hated Stamp Act.

The Stamp Act was a way for Britain to collect tax money from the colonies. Taxed goods included newspapers, liquor licenses, law licenses, legal papers, and playing cards. Each of these items would require a tax stamp. The higher the cost of the stamp, the less money the shopkeepers made.

When King George III of Britain brought an end to the Stamp Act in 1766, everyone celebrated. In taverns, men drank toasts to one another. Church bells chimed. Fireworks exploded. Later, Phillis wrote a poem remembering the event. This time she wrote only two versions. She called it "To the King's Most Excellent Majesty." She praised the king, saying, "A monarch's smile can set his subjects free."

Like everyone else in Boston, Phillis hoped that King George would continue to listen to the colonists' cries for freedom. As a slave, she understood the value of freedom even more.

Blood in the Streets

As they struggled against British rule, many people in Boston became more aware of the importance of freedom and the harshness of slavery. Some people worked to rid the colonies of slavery. Others spoke against the idea of slavery but did little to stop it. In May of 1766, several Bostonians asked their representatives not only to outlaw the purchase of slaves but to do away with slavery completely. The legislature took no action.

But Phillis took action. With her quill pen in hand, she tackled one subject after another. At the age of thirteen, she composed what was to become one of her best-known poems. She called it "To the University of Cambridge." She had no doubt heard about the fuss some Harvard students had made because the kitchen staff had served them stale butter.

Phillis could not believe her ears. Were the students not grateful simply to have the chance to study and learn at a university? In her poem, Phillis advised the students to use their chance to learn everything they could. Phillis would surely have given anything to have such an opportunity. And here they were complaining about butter! She might have plenty of pens, paper, and books—and she was thankful for them. But she knew that because she was black, a woman, and a slave, she would never attend college.

Phillis always paid close attention to what was going on around her. That was how she found ideas for her poems. In the fall of 1767, John Wheatley invited two gentlemen—Mr. Hussey and Mr. Coffin—to join him for dinner. During the meal, they told of their narrow escape from death in a storm off Cape Cod. Phillis overheard the story.

That evening, she went to her room, but she could not sleep. Like the winds of the storm, the words of a poem swirled in her head. She wrote and rewrote, late into the night, until the verses pleased her.

The next morning, Phillis showed the poem to Susanna, who thought it was good enough to be printed in a newspaper. Phillis probably rewrote the poem several more times. Then, with Susanna's urging, the *Newport Mercury* published "On Messrs

Hussey and Coffin" on December 21, 1767. Now people all over the colonies could appreciate the work of this talented young poet. Phillis and Susanna were overjoyed to see one of Phillis's poems in print— along with Phillis's name.

By the fall of 1768, King George was quite certain that the colonists were not happy being ruled by Britain. But he still wanted to control the colonies. The Stamp Act had failed, so he tried a new approach. On September 30, 1768, British soldiers landed in Boston harbor. Their ships' cannons were loaded and ready for battle.

The next day, seven hundred British troops marched down King Street to Boston Common, a large park in the center of the city. Soldiers in red coats, their swords drawn, led the procession. Phillis, along with the other people of Boston, stood silently and watched. Phillis composed a poem describing the events of that day. She called it "On the Arrival of the Ships of War, and Landing of the Troops."

Tension increased as four thousand British soldiers took over the town. Young boys taunted the redcoats, calling them lobsterbacks. "Lobsters for sale!" they would tease. It wasn't easy for the soldiers, either. Many were young. They were not paid well. And they were homesick.

Some of the colonists believed that Britain should have control over them. One of those was Ebenezer Richardson. On the evening of February 22, 1770, a group of boys surrounded Richardson's house. Rock-filled snowballs crashed through his windows. As the noise swelled, he took out his musket and fired into the mob. Eleven swanshot pellets hit and killed eleven-year-old Christopher Snider.

Nearly all of Boston turned out for young Snider's funeral. Despite her asthma, Phillis wrapped a shawl around her thin shoulders and shivered in the cold along with everyone else. Then she marched home, took her pen in hand, and wrote a poem about the incident. In the poem, she sided with the rebel colonists against the British, the "hated brood." She called Christopher Snider "the first martyr for the cause."

As the winter of 1770 wore on, tempers heated on both sides. On the evening of March 5, a mantle of snow and ice covered the city. At the corner of King Street and Exchange Lane, only blocks from the Wheatley home, a British soldier kept watch in front of the Customs House. Around eight o'clock, a young boy started an argument with the soldier. Before anyone knew what happened, everyone was shouting. In the scuffle, a gun went off. Suddenly, the soldiers were firing into the crowd.

Phillis heard the musket blasts. She heard every church bell in Boston ringing, too. When the shooting stopped, three men lay dead. One was Crispus Attucks, a fugitive slave who had run away from his master twenty years earlier and had never been caught. Phillis set down the events of the Boston Massacre, as it came to be called, in a poem titled "On the Affray in King Street, on the Evening of the 5th of March."

Soon the British troops left Boston, but they did not go back to Britain. They simply moved to Castle William, an island in Boston harbor, and there they sat.

Her Curiosity
Led Her to It

In the fall of 1770, Phillis wrote a poem about a preacher she admired—the Reverend George White-field. Whitefield had been one of the most powerful speakers in all the colonies. Once when he was speaking at the New South Church, the crowd became so excited that five people were trampled to death.

Whitefield died suddenly of an asthma attack on September 30 in Massachusetts. He had been a generous man, raising money to build an orphanage and working to help the homeless. Yet he defended slavery on Biblical grounds. He had, in fact, purchased some fifty slaves to build the orphanage.

Nevertheless, Phillis was fond of Whitefield, and she quickly composed a poem praising him. It began: "Hail happy saint, on thine immortal throne, Possest [Possessed] of glory, life and bliss unknown; We hear no more the music of thy tongue."

The week after Whitefield died, the *Massachusetts Spy* advertised for sale "An Elegiac Poem, on the Death of the Celebrated Divine…By PHILLIS, a Servant girl of 17 years of Age, Belonging to Mr. J. WHEATLEY…but 9 Years in this Country from Africa." The poem was printed in Boston, New York, and Philadelphia, and also in Britain. No one knows for certain, but Susanna probably paid to have the poem printed. The printer may have paid for it himself, knowing that Whitefield's popularity would sell the poem. In any case, Phillis's fame now spread beyond Boston and even beyond Massachusetts.

Susanna encouraged Phillis to send a copy of the poem to Susanna's friend the Countess of Huntingdon in Britain. Reverend Whitefield had been the countess's private clergyman. The countess was a wealthy woman who gave much of her fortune to charitable and religious causes. Because they knew and admired many of the same ministers, Susanna and the countess had become friends.

Phillis enclosed this note with the poem: "The occasion of my addressing your Ladiship will, I hope, apologize for this my boldness in doing it: it is to enclose a few lines on the decease of your worthy chaplain, the Rev'd Mr. Whitefield, in the loss of whom I sincerely sympathize with your Ladiship."

On January 31, 1771, Mary Wheatley left her parents' home to marry the Reverend John Lathrop, pastor of the Old North Church in Boston. He was called the "Revolutionary Preacher" because his sermons often attacked the British. When Phillis visited John and Mary at their home in the North End, the servants were taken aback. They had never before served tea to a black woman. But Phillis's wit and charm soon put everyone at ease.

Like his sister Mary, Nathaniel Wheatley was moving on. When John Wheatley retired in July 1771, Nathaniel bought all of his father's property, including the mansion on King Street. But instead of living in the house, he married into a well-to-do British family and spent most of his time in London.

With Nathaniel and Mary gone, Susanna spent even more time with Phillis. She rejoiced with her eighteen-year-old servant when, on August 18, 1771, Phillis was baptized at the Old South Church. This was the church she had attended since arriving in America. Now she would be an official member. Religion continued to be an important part of Phillis's life, as it was for most colonists. The churches, like the taverns, were the gathering places of the town.

Phillis had joined the Old South Church even though the Wheatleys belonged to the New South.

Old South was closer to the Wheatley home. Because Phillis continued to suffer from poor health, Susanna decided she should attend services there.

Since Phillis was a slave, the baptismal ceremony took place at the end rather than during the church service. In the Old South Church, as in every other church in Boston, black people always sat in the back, or more likely, in the second-floor gallery.

Meanwhile, Phillis was not looking forward to another bitter cold Massachusetts winter. That was when her asthma attacks were the worst. But Phillis was too busy writing and rewriting to let health problems stop her.

She composed one elegy after another. Phillis especially liked to use her poems to give comfort to someone who had lost a loved one. Her words carried a popular message—that life on earth was merely a stop on the way to heaven. In one poem about the death of a child, Phillis told the parents, "Freed from a world of sin, and snares, and pain, why would you wish your daughter back again?"

By the fall of 1772, Phillis's fame as a poet had spread beyond the colonies. But Susanna wanted even more notice of Phillis's writing. Though she would not have wished to be prideful, Phillis probably liked the attention, too.

Susanna saw to it that Phillis met powerful people who could promote her work. Sometimes John and Susanna would invite friends to their home. Phillis, with her poetry, would provide the entertainment.

Other times, Phillis was invited to people's homes to read her poetry. One day Susanna arranged for Phillis to meet Mrs. Eunice Fitch, the wife of the wealthy merchant who owned the slave ship *Phillis*. At teatime, Mrs. Fitch insisted that Phillis sit with the family. Mrs. Fitch's daughters had probably never dreamed that they would sit down for tea with a slave. But they later reported that the conversation with Phillis was so lively that they "forgot her color."

Like the Fitches, Susanna saw Phillis as "better" than other black people. Once, when Phillis was visiting a well-known Boston family, the weather turned bad and Susanna sent Prince, the Wheatleys' driver, to fetch her. As the carriage approached the house, Susanna exclaimed, "Do but look at the saucy varlet —if he hasn't the impudence to sit upon the same seat with my Phillis." Phillis must have felt caught between two worlds—not allowed to associate with the other slaves and yet not free, like the white people with whom she mingled.

Phillis did have one friend of her own, but she did not live nearby. Her name was Obour Tanner and she lived in Newport, Rhode Island, as the servant of James Tanner. The two women probably met when the Wheatleys visited Newport, a popular resort area. Phillis and Obour sent letters back and forth, but they did not get to see each other often.

For Susanna, it was not enough that Phillis's writing had been published in newspapers. She wanted to see Phillis's work in a book. Before a book could be published, people had to subscribe to it—they had to agree to buy it when it was printed. A two-hundred-page book required three hundred subscribers.

During the winter of 1772, Phillis again battled asthma and possibly tuberculosis. In spite of her ill health, she chose—with Susanna's help—twenty-eight of her best verses. Then Susanna helped her put an advertisement in the *Boston Censor* listing the titles of the poems.

Phillis announced that a book of poems could be purchased "handsomely bound and lettered" for four shillings or "stitched in blue" for three shillings. Both Phillis and Susanna were disappointed when not enough people subscribed and the book could not be published.

But now Phillis and Susanna were determined to see Phillis's poems in a book. If the people of Boston did not care enough about Phillis's poems to have them printed, maybe the people of Britain would. Phillis removed the anti-British poems and selected others that favored the British. She also changed the titles of several poems to make them more general. For example, "To Mrs. Leonard on the Death of her Husband" became "To a Lady on the Death of her Husband."

Susanna told Phillis to write to the Countess of Huntingdon to ask for her support of the book. If anyone had the money and influence to get Phillis's poems published as a book, the countess did. Then Susanna wrote to Archibald Bell, London's foremost bookseller and printer. Bell replied that since Phillis was a slave, he needed proof that she had indeed written the poems. That was not a problem.

On October 8, 1772, Susanna gathered eighteen of Boston's most reputable citizens. They included Governor Thomas Hutchinson, John Hancock, and Reverend Samuel Cooper. The men questioned Phillis, although they all knew of her talent. Phillis graciously answered all their questions. Then the men signed a paper saying "that the Poems specified in the following Page were (as we verily believe) written by Phillis." And further, "She has been examined by some of the best Judges, and is thought qualified to write them."

31

It was no secret that most of the men who signed the document owned slaves themselves. One of the signers, Thomas Hubbard, even sold slaves. Phillis knew him because he was a deacon at Old South Church. These men saw Phillis as an exception, and they supported her efforts to publish a book.

In November, Captain Robert Calef sailed John Wheatley's ship, the *London Packet,* to Britain. Before he left, John gave him the manuscript containing Phillis's poems. John also wrote a letter attesting to Phillis's brilliance, saying, "As to her Writing, her own Curiosity led her to it." When Calef arrived in London, he delivered the pages straight to Archibald Bell's shop at No. 8 Aldgate Street.

Near the first of December, 1772, Archibald Bell called on the Countess of Huntingdon and brought the poems. As he read them to her, the countess stopped him from time to time and said, "Do you not think this is very fine?" and "Do read another."

The countess vowed that Philis's poems would be printed as a book. And she was delighted that Phillis wanted to dedicate the book to her. But, she said, a picture of Phillis must appear in the front of the volume. And who better to produce a portrait than another poet and slave who was also an artist. Scipio Moorhead of Boston was soon hired to create a pen-

and-ink drawing of Phillis. Susanna thought the picture was so lifelike that she said, "See, look at my Phillis, does she not seem as though she would speak to me!"

Cold weather always made Phillis's asthma worse, but the winter of 1772 nearly killed her. Susanna was worried. She wrote to the Countess of Huntingdon on April 30, 1773: "Phillis being in a poor state of Health, the Physicians advise to the sea air." Nathaniel Wheatley was traveling to Britain on business, and it was decided that Phillis would come along. Susanna asked the countess to see that Phillis stayed in a Christian home and to help her buy new clothes. Susanna sent money with Phillis, along with a note that said, "I like she should be dress'd plain."

Phillis was overwhelmed by the news of this new adventure. As far as she knew, slaves were not allowed to travel much within the colonies. And here she was, journeying to another country.

In London, she would meet the Countess of Huntingdon and other important people. But she was worried, too. Would Susanna be all right without her? Her health had not been good. As Phillis packed for her trip, a new poem began to form in her head.

4

Farewell to America

Before she left for Britain, Phillis sat down at her writing table, picked up her quill pen, and wrote a poem called "Farewell to America." In it she spoke of the beauty of New England, calling it a "flow'ry plain." She wrote that she hoped the voyage would restore her "rosy hue." She voiced her sadness at leaving with these words:

Susanna mourns, nor can I bear
    To see the crystal show'r,
Or mark the tender falling tear
    At sad departure's hour.

Nineteen-year-old Phillis was now so well known that newspapers printed "Farewell to America" and also reported on her upcoming trip to Britain. Writers called her "the extraordinary negro poetess," and "the ingenious negro poet."

With hugs and tears, Phillis sailed for London on May 8, 1773. She arrived five weeks later. On June 27, she sent a letter to the Countess of Huntingdon to tell her she had arrived. "I should think my self very happy in seeing your Ladyship," Phillis wrote, "and if you was so desirous of the Image of the Author as to propose it for a Frontispiece I flatter myself that you would accept the Reality." However, the seventy-one-year old countess was ill and could not leave her estate in South Wales. Phillis was disappointed that she would not be able to thank the countess in person for all her help.

Still, Phillis kept busy during her stay in London. The countess saw to that. A chaperon showed Phillis around famous places such as Westminster Abbey and the British Museum. At the Tower of London, Phillis stared in amazement at the jewels, the crowns, and the baptismal font of the royal family.

If she had a spare moment, Phillis read over her poems to make sure the words were just right. Since they were going to be printed in a book, they had to be perfect. Phillis probably enjoyed imagining the soft leather of the book's cover.

But Phillis had little time for daydreaming. She was too busy meeting many of Britain's most powerful people. Her social calendar read like a who's who of London. One day she chatted with Lord Dartmouth, who had the title "His Majesty's Principal Secretary of State for North America." She spent an enjoyable afternoon visiting with Mrs. Palmer, a well-known poet. Another day she was entertained by Dr. Solander's tales of his journeys around the world.

Benjamin Franklin was in London at the time as a spokesperson for the American colonies. Phillis was delighted when Franklin visited her and said he would do anything he could to help her. Phillis could not believe her eyes when the Lord Mayor of London handed her an elegantly bound copy of *Paradise Lost,* a classic of English literature.

The Earl of Dartmouth, when he learned of Phillis's love of Alexander Pope's poetry, gave her money to buy the entire set of Pope's works. For the first time in her life, Phillis felt the thrill of holding in her hands books that she owned.

Meanwhile, back in Boston, Susanna continued her efforts to promote Phillis's writing. The week after Phillis left, Susanna sent a copy of "Farewell to America" by ship to the editor of the *London Chronicle.* The editor printed the poem in the July 1–3 issue.

In London, Phillis had the opportunity to watch as Archibald Bell set into type the poems she had written. What had once been merely a manuscript was now becoming a book. It would be called *Poems on Various Subjects, Religious and Moral.* The work might have gone more quickly if Phillis had not been present. She was so precise in her writing that she went over every word many times.

Phillis had an appointment to meet King George while she was in Britain. However, in mid-July she received a letter saying that Susanna was sick and wanted Phillis to come home. After only four weeks in London, Phillis set sail for New England on Thursday, July 22, 1773.

When she got home, Phillis found Susanna very ill. She wrote to a friend in London, "When I first arriv'd at home my mistress was so bad as not to be expected to live above two or three days, but through the goodness of God, she is still alive."

Despite Susanna's illness, Phillis enjoyed telling the Wheatleys and other friends about her exciting trip. She quickly wrote to Obour Tanner about how kind everyone had been to her. However, she told Obour, the trip had not improved her health: "I am at present indisposed by a cold, and since my arrival have been visited by the asthma."

Although Phillis was sick, and she was taking care of Susanna, she sat down, picked up her pen and wrote another elegy. This one was in memory of Scipio Moorhead's master, the Reverend John Moorhead. In doing this, she hoped also to honor Scipio and to thank him for painting her portrait.

For weeks Phillis was occupied with sickness. But she could not help noticing that Boston was still in turmoil. King George was still trying to control the colonists, and many of them were still rebelling.

Food became scarce. Phillis realized that selling books to people who did not have food was not going to be easy. And Susanna was in no condition to help her. Phillis asked Obour for her help in finding American buyers for her book. "I enclose Proposals for my book," she wrote, "and beg you'd use your interest to get subscriptions, as it is for my benefit."

In September, *Poems on Various Subjects* was finally published and advertised for sale in London. The *London Chronicle* on September 16, 1773, announced: "Dedicated, by permission, to the Right Hon. the Countess of Huntingdon. This Day was published . . . adorned with an elegant engraved likeness of the Author, A Volume of POEMS, on various Subjects, RELIGIOUS and MORAL. By PHILLIS WHEATLEY, Negro Servant to Mr. John Wheatley of

Boston/London." At just twenty years old, Phillis became the first black American, and only the second American woman, to publish a book. Copies of the book were not yet available in the colonies, but Phillis must have been thrilled and proud.

Soon after *Poems on Various Subjects* was published in London, reviewers praised it. *Westminister Magazine* said: "It would be unfair to deaden so young and so promising a poetical plant with the Frost of Criticism." Seeing Phillis's talent, the *Monthly Review* of London jabbed at the colonists for practicing slavery. "We are much concerned to find that this ingenious young woman is yet a slave."

John Wheatley may have read those reviews and taken them to heart. In a letter dated October 18, 1773, Phillis announced: "Since my return to America my Master, has at the desire of my friends in England given me my freedom." John Wheatley may also have been following the custom that a slave who set foot in Britain would be free.

In any case, Phillis was now released from slavery. Phillis may have had her freedom, but she had little else. She was still living in the Wheatley home and caring for Susanna. But she knew that when Susanna died, she would no longer be needed. Then she might not have a home.

Phillis knew, too, that the time was coming when she would have to rely on income from her books to survive. She realized how difficult it was going to be to support herself. Still, simply having her freedom had given her a new confidence. She expressed her feelings in a letter to the Reverend Samson Occom. He was the popular preacher to whom she had written when she was younger. "In every human Breast," she wrote, "God has implanted a Principle, which we call Love of Freedom; it is impatient of Oppression, and pants for Deliverance." Her letter was reprinted in nearly a dozen newspapers throughout the colonies.

Freedom was on the minds of Bostonians, too, and the city was still in an uproar. When the British Parliament passed a law meant to force the colonists to buy British tea and to pay a tax on it, colonial merchants were furious. On Friday, December 17, over seven thousand people gathered at Old South Church. When the church was full, the rest stood outside in the freezing rain. British tea must not be allowed into Boston harbor, everyone said. "To the docks!" they shouted. At Griffin's Wharf, they poured 342 chests of tea into the harbor.

When King George heard what had happened, he was furious. "The New England colonies are in a state of rebellion," he said. "Blows must decide whether they are to be subject to this country or independent." The colonies were moving toward war.

Despite the unrest, Phillis continued to try to sell her books. In January 1774, three hundred copies of *Poems on Various Subjects* arrived from London. The *Boston Gazette* advertised the books' arrival and asked subscribers to come purchase their copies, which cost "Two Shillings Sewed or Two Shillings and Six-pence neatly bound." In the advertisement, Phillis was now described as "a Negro Girl" rather than a servant girl.

In a letter to Colonel David Wooster, Phillis once again asked for help selling books. She told him that she would receive half the price of each book sold. She needed his help, she said, because "it is the Chief I have to depend upon."

Phillis's friend Obour Tanner had sold some of Phillis's books. Phillis appreciated Obour's efforts and wrote to thank her. She said, "Your tenderness for my welfare demands my gratitude."

For seven months, Phillis nursed Susanna as she lay dying. Phillis was at her bedside on a March morning in 1774, when sixty-five-year-old Susanna died. Two days later, Phillis walked, head bowed, with John, Mary, and the other mourners carrying

Susanna's body to the Old Granary Burial Grounds. At the cemetery, Phillis listened quietly while John Hancock remembered Susanna's virtues.

Phillis had lost not only a friend, but someone akin to a mother. In a letter to Obour Tanner dated March 21, 1774, Phillis said, "Let us imagine the loss of a parent, sister or brother, the tenderness of all these were united in her. I was a poor little outcast & a stranger when she took me in: not only into the house, but I presently became a sharer in her most tender affections."

Phillis would surely have written a poem to honor Susanna had she not forbidden Phillis to do so. Susanna was so humble that she did not want her good deeds mentioned even after her death.

Phillis stayed on in the Wheatley mansion for a time to care for John. Nathaniel now lived in England with his family, and Mary was busy with five babies under five years old. Phillis wrote to her friend John Thornton, "I feel like one forsaken by her parent in a desolate wilderness." Although Phillis had a few friends in Boston, she was now on her own.

So Favored by the Muses

On May 10, 1774, the people of Boston got word of their punishment for the tea-dumping incident, or Boston Tea Party, as some called it. As of June 1, the British would close the port of Boston. No ships could leave or enter the harbor. That meant no food or fuel could be brought into the city except by land. King George would starve the colonists. That would teach them to obey.

Luckily, before the harbor closed, Phillis received a shipment of three hundred more copies of her book from Archibald Bell in London. Now she needed to sell them. She placed a notice in the *Boston Evening Post and Advertiser,* listing the work as that of "Phillis Wheatley, A Negro Girl, Printed for the benefit of the Author."

Now 4,500 British soldiers were living in Boston.

The colonists had to lodge them in their homes. They did not like that, and the soldiers were not happy either. Fights broke out in taverns and on the streets. The soldiers destroyed the Old South Church, where Phillis had been baptized. They tore out the pulpit and pews and used them for firewood. They exercised their horses on the dirt floor.

With so much destruction going on, anyone who could leave Boston soon did. John Wheatley moved in with relatives in nearby Chelsea. Mary Lathrop traveled with her husband, John, to Providence, Rhode Island, where he took over as minister of a church there. Phillis went along to nurse Mary back to health. Mary had given birth to five children in less than five years, and four of them had died.

By April 1775, the Revolutionary War between the colonies and Britain had officially begun. In June, Phillis heard the news that George Washington had been appointed commander in chief of the colonial troops, known as the Continental Army. He had set up headquarters across the Charles River in Cambridge, and seventeen thousand colonists had joined him. Phillis liked what General Washington was doing to try to oust the British. On October 26, 1775, she wrote to tell him so. Not surprisingly, she enclosed a poem praising General Washington.

Touched by Phillis's words, Washington wrote back to her on February 28, 1776. He thanked Phillis for her "elegant lines" and invited her to visit his headquarters. He wrote, "I shall be happy to see a person so favored by the muses." (That meant he thought she was a good poet.)

Phillis was quick to take General Washington up on his offer. When would she have another chance like this? In March, Phillis made the trip to Cambridge. She waited in line with politicians and businessmen to see the great general. Washington, who himself owned slaves, took thirty minutes out of his busy schedule to talk with her.

By now it was obvious that with the colonies working together, the British could not take over Boston. The Continental Army had gathered not only troops but also ammunition from all the colonies. With all those big guns pointed at them, the British saw they were defeated. So on March 17, 1776, the British soldiers packed up and left Massachusetts. The war continued in the other colonies.

When Phillis returned to Boston, she found most of the town demolished. What the soldiers had not ruined, they had taken with them. The Wheatley mansion was gone, destroyed by a bomb. Because goods were scarce, prices were extremely high.

One man sold his cow only to find he had to pay the same amount for a goose. A loaf of bread now cost two shillings—the same price as Phillis's book. A bushel of potatoes cost ten shillings.

Phillis continued to try to sell her books to support herself. But with food expensive and in short supply, it was not the best time to be selling books of poetry. Phillis lived for a time with Susanna's niece, who was a widow. The woman's son had been killed in the war, and she did not have much money. Still, she gladly gave Phillis a home for a while.

6

Fair Freedom's Charms

On Valentine's Day, 1778, John Wheatley wrote his will. He did not mention Phillis. He named his son-in-law, John Lathrop, to handle his affairs when he died. He had already given or sold most of his property to Nathaniel, and he left the rest of it to Mary. Perhaps John was already ill when he made out his will, because a month later, on March 12, 1778, he died.

Now Phillis had no home and no family. Nathaniel and Mary had lives of their own. Phillis thought about a man she had once met named John Peters. He had delivered a letter to her from Obour. At the time she had told Obour she found him "complaisant and agreeable."

Someone who knew Peters described him as a "fluent writer, a ready speaker, and an intelligent man." Before becoming a lawyer, Peters had been a grocer on Queen Street. He may have also been a baker, a barber, and a doctor. As a lawyer, he called himself Doctor Peters. According to some, Peters was handsome and well-mannered. Others thought he put on airs by wearing a wig and carrying a cane.

In either case, Phillis liked him. On April 1, 1778, Boston newspapers announced the wedding of Phillis Wheatley and John Peters, "free Negroes." The couple lived on Queen Street in Boston, at least for a while. The house was probably not a mansion, but it must have been fairly large. Peters paid a high amount of taxes on it.

Somewhere in that house on Queen Street, Phillis must have had a writing table, because write she did. On July 15, 1778, Phillis sent the poem "On the Death of General Wooster" to his wife to console her. Wooster was the former colonel who had generously helped Phillis sell some of her books. He had died in a battle with the British.

Now, with her freedom, Phillis found the courage to express more of her feelings about slavery. In the poem for Mrs. Wooster, Phillis wove together the ideas of freedom for the colonies and freedom for all

African people. She spoke about "fair freedom's charms." She wondered how the Americans could value their own freedom and still "hold in bondage Afric's blameless race."

In her letter to Mrs. Wooster, Phillis also asked her to return any of Phillis's books that she had not sold. Phillis wrote, "I can easily dispose of them here for 12 shillings." This was about six times the book's original price.

In the fall of the year, Phillis felt the pain of yet another death. Her friend and teacher, Mary Wheatley Lathrop, died on September 24, 1778. She was thirty-five years old. Phillis did not write a poem in memory of Mary. Like her mother Susanna, Mary probably asked Phillis not to write about her.

Around this time, Phillis became pregnant with her first child. To honor this event, she wrote a prayer. In it, she asked for the strength to deliver a healthy child. The prayer is dated June 13, 1779, but she did not record the date of the baby's birth.

Sometime after the birth of her child, Phillis tried to put together a second book of poems. Beginning October 30, 1779, she advertised in the *Boston Evening Post and General Advertiser* for subscriptions. The book would consist of thirty-three poems and thirteen letters.

Phillis hoped that the book would sell for twelve shillings, "neatly Bound & Lettered," and nine shillings "sew'd in blue paper." She took Benjamin Franklin up on his offer of help by dedicating her proposed second volume of poems to him. Yet even Benjamin Franklin's name did not attract the needed subscribers. War with the British had left the people of Boston without extra money to spend on books.

For the next few years, Phillis and her husband and child seemed to disappear. They probably moved to Wilmington, Massachusetts, north of Boston. Despite her fragile health, Phillis gave birth to two more children there.

As Phillis and her family struggled, the Revolutionary War came to an end. On October 19, 1781, British troops surrendered to the Continental Army at Yorktown, Virginia. Bostonians marked the end of the fighting with bells ringing and cannons booming. Town officials marched from the State House to the Old South Church for speeches and songs and then to Faneuil Hall for an elegant meal.

Nathaniel Wheatley died on April 3, 1783, in London. He had done well in business, and he left an ample inheritance for his wife and three daughters. However, he did not mention Phillis in his will.

Sometime after the war ended, Phillis returned to

Boston with her family. The town was still a sorry sight because of the war. Peters opened a shop on Prince Street. But the store went broke, and Peters ended up in debtors' prison. Phillis tried to make the best of her situation by washing sheets in a boarding-house. This kind of work did not help her asthma. With the little money she made, she was barely able to feed her children.

But no matter what happened, Phillis kept on writing. She wrote a poem on the death of Reverend Samuel Cooper. Reverend Cooper had baptized Phillis into the Old South Church, and he had always encouraged her writing.

In February 1784, Phillis wrote a poem about the signing of the peace treaty between the United States and Britain. She called it "Liberty and Peace." The poem celebrated the American victory, and its final lines described a hopeful future: "To every Realm shall *Peace* her Charms display, And Heavenly *Freedom* spread her golden ray."

While Phillis was happy that the colonists had defeated the British, she must have also felt a deep sadness. Her life was becoming more and more difficult. Her husband was in prison. She was so weak she could barely hold a pen. And still she wrote.

In September, the *Boston Magazine* printed

Phillis's last published poem. It was an elegy, like so many of her other poems. This time it was written to a mother and father on the death of their infant son. The magazine's editor wrote Phillis a note saying that the poem would be part of a book if there were enough subscribers. Sadly, there were not enough, and this book of poems was never published.

By December of 1784, Phillis lay sick and dying in the boardinghouse where she worked. Two of her children had died, and the third was near death. Her husband was not with her. He was probably still in prison on December 5, the day both his wife and child passed away.

The *Boston Independent Chronicle and Universal Advertiser* for December 9 ran this notice: "Last Lord's day died Mrs. Phillis Peters (formerly Phillis Wheatley) aged 31, known to the literary world by her celebrated Miscellaneous Poems. Her funeral is to be this afternoon, at four o'clock, from the house lately repaired by Mr. Todd, nearly opposite Dr. Bullfinch's, at West Boston, where her friends and ac-quaintances are desired to attend."

No one knows who attended Phillis's funeral or where she was buried. It was customary at that time for black people to be laid to rest on Copp's Hill, overlooking Boston harbor. However, her body may have been placed, along with Susanna's, in the Old Granary Burial Grounds.

Sometime after Phillis died, John Peters sold the books Phillis had received as gifts on her trip to London. Then on February 10, 1785, a notice appeared in the *Boston Independent Chronicle and Universal Advertiser:* "The person who borrowed a volume of manuscript poems . . . of Phillis Peters, formerly Phillis Wheatley, deceased, would very much oblige her husband, John Peters, by returning it immediately, as the whole of her works are intended to be published." Peters got the manuscript back, but he never published the poems.

Afterword

Poems on Various Subjects, Religious and Moral was published for the first time in the United States in 1786, two years after Phillis's death. Since then, the book has been reprinted more than a dozen times. At an auction in 1984, a copy signed by Phillis sold for nearly two thousand dollars. A copy of the book is on display at the Old South Meeting House (formerly Old South Church) in Boston.

During the 1800s, Phillis and her poetry were frequently mentioned by people who sought to abolish slavery. Charlotte L. Forten, the granddaughter of a well-known abolitionist, read Phillis's poems when she was sixteen years old. In 1854 she commented in her diary, "She was a wonderfully gifted woman, and many of her poems are very beautiful. Her character and genius afford a striking proof of the falseness of the assertion made by some that hers is an inferior race."

In the twentieth century, Phillis has again been recognized as an important American poet. She is sometimes called the mother of black literature. The poet Nikki Giovanni once wrote, "We have a line of strong poets. Wheatley, by her life style, was a strong woman intent on survival."

The memory of Phillis Wheatley survives. Every day, more and more people become aware of her extraordinary accomplishments and of the part she played in the history of Boston and the United States. Her memory is kept alive by organizations such as the Boston Women's Heritage Trail and the Boston National Historical Park. The Massachusetts Historical Society sometimes displays a writing table that belonged to Phillis.

Although we may never uncover all the details of Phillis's life, scholars continue to search for lost letters and poems that will help us know this great American poet.

Bibliography

Forbes, Esther. *Paul Revere and the World He Lived In.* Boston: Houghton Mifflin, 1942.

Odell, Margaretta Matilda. *Memoirs and Poems of Phillis Wheatley.* 3rd edition. Boston, 1838. Reprinted by Mnemosyne Publishing Co., Miami, FL, 1969.

Rawley, James A. "The World of Phillis Wheatley," *New England Quarterly* 50, no. 4, December 1977.

Renfro, G. Herbert. *Life and Works of Phillis Wheatley.* Freeport, NY: Books for Libraries Press, 1916.

Richmond, Merle A. *Bid the Vassal Soar.* Washington, DC: Howard University Press, 1974.

Robinson, William H. *Critical Essays on Phillis Wheatley.* Boston: G. K. Hall, 1982.

Robinson, William H. *Phillis Wheatley and Her Writings.* New York: Garland, 1984.

Robinson, William H. *Phillis Wheatley: A Bio-bibliography.* Boston: G. K. Hall, 1981.

Shields, John C., ed. *The Collected Works of Phillis Wheatley.* New York: Oxford University Press, 1988.

Index

About the Author

Maryann N. Weidt was a children's librarian for twenty years. She lives with her husband and children in Duluth, Minnesota. She is also the author of *Oh, the Places He Went: A Story about Dr. Seuss, Stateswoman to the World: A Story about Eleanor Roosevelt,* and *Mr. Blue Jeans: A Story about Levi Strauss,* all published by Carolrhoda Books.

About the Illustrator

Mary O'Keefe Young studied art at Parsons School of Design in New York City and has been an illustrator for thirteen years. In addition to illustration, Mrs. Young enjoys photography, sewing costumes, and painting portraits. Raised in Larchmont, New York, she now lives in nearby White Plains with her husband and three children.